ISBN 978-1-334-48739-2
PIBN 10685951

For support please visit www.forgottenbooks.com

English
Français
Deutsche
Italiano
Español
Português

www.forgottenbooks.com

Mythology Photography **Fiction**
Fishing Christianity **Art** Cooking
Essays Buddhism Freemasonry
Medicine **Biology** Music **Ancient**
Egypt Evolution Carpentry Physics
Dance Geology **Mathematics** Fitness
Shakespeare **Folklore** Yoga Marketing
Confidence Immortality Biographies
Poetry **Psychology** Witchcraft
Electronics Chemistry History **Law**
Accounting **Philosophy** Anthropology
Alchemy Drama Quantum Mechanics
Atheism Sexual Health **Ancient History**
Entrepreneurship Languages Sport
Paleontology Needlework Islam
Metaphysics Investment Archaeology
Parenting Statistics Criminology
Motivational

THE

British SEAMAN's

LETTER,

ADDRESS'D

To the Free-Holders, Voters, and all the good Subjects of *GREAT-BRITAIN*.

ADDRESS'D

THE

British SEAMAN's

LETTER,

ADDRESS'D

To the Free-Holders, Voters, and all the good Subjects of G R E A T-B R I T A I N :

WITH

Some OBSERVATIONS on the suspending of the *TRIENNIAL ACT.*

From on Board the SOVEREIGN, April *the* 17th, 1716.

L O N D O N :

Printed, and Sold by *J. Roberts*, near the *Oxford-Arms* in *Warwick-Lane.* 1716.

(Price Three-pence.)

THE

British SEAMAN's

LETTER.

Greeting you all moſt heàrtily,

OUT of a ſteady, unbiaſs'd, generous, and ſincere Love of my Country, I preſume, at this Juncture, whilſt there are ſtill amongſt us ſome horrid

Remains

Remains of a late bafe, infamous, and treafonable Rebellion, which, as it was, at firft, begun, and carry'd on, by bloody minded *Papifts*, and *Jacobites*, at Home, fpirited on, and fupported by *Romifh Votaries*, Slaves and Idolaters from Abroad, and is yet nurs'd and kept alive, upon the hopes of the like Springs, and Affiftance for the future, to offer to your mature, deliberate Judgments, my honeft, and worthy *Proteftant Countrymen*, the fol-

and juft Obfervations.

You can't but hear the daily Clamours, and villainous Suggeftions of the *Popifh Traiterous Fiction* againft the beft of Kings, and moft deferving Parliaments, and Miniftry; fuch, as at one and the fame time, this Nation was hardly ever blefs'd withal; and

term

term His tender, and unprecedented Clemency, and Mercy, to the moſt evil, obnoxious, ſanguinary Wretches that ever exiſted ; Monſters, taken in open Arms, in a concerted, grand Aſſociation, and Rebellion ; a Maſſacre, a delighting in Blood. Oh baſe, and ungrateful !

Was not the Deſign of theſe unnatural *Rebels* in favour of a moſt notorious *Impoſtor*, and *Popiſh Pretender* to the Crown, Dignity, and Government of the *Britiſh* Realms, a ſervile Slave to *Rome* and *France?* And in order to Depoſe, and Murder our moſt ſacred Sovereign, and Royal Family? Root up, and totally to Extirpate our moſt Holy Church, the Darlings of Heaven, with all the worthy Members of the ſame, in manifeſt Violation of the many wholſome Acts of

Parli-

Parliament subsisting ? And what is extreamly corrupt, and most detestably odious, hardly to be believ'd, but alas, too true ; that some Professors of, and Pretenders to this sacred, and National Establishment, belonging to *Rochester, Holbourn, Oxford, Tyburn, Newgate,* the *Tower,* the *Fleet* and *Sea* ; not that of which, I thank God, I am an honest Member, have principally, chiefly, and diligently stirr'd up, fomented, aided, countenanc'd, and abetted these damnable, curs'd Insurrections, and Rebellion with all their dire, and dreadful Consequences ?

Was not the Design of these *Traytors* to undermine, and blow up the best constituted Government both in Church, and State, on Earth, that ever was fram'd by God and Man ?

Was

Was not the Design to unravel the whole Texture of our Laws, sacred and political? To sink, and emerge our Liberties and Properties? Divest us of our Estates? Give up our Trade to foreign *Papists*? Reduce us to Want and Beggary? Force our Wives and Daughters? Massacre the Major Part, and leave the Remainder to the whole Enjoyment of Rags, and Wooden Shoes? All submitting to the infernal Rage of *French* Dragoons?

Sure, my brave Countrymen, you can't, but with the utmost Horror, and Dread, look back, and read the greatest, and most valuable Historians of the last Century, there you'l find above Two Hundred Thousand Protestants, without Distinction of Age, Sex, or Dignity, murder'd in cool Blood, by *Villains* of the same Stamp,

B   same

same Principles, same Pretences with these late horrid *Rebels* ; and for no other Reason, but becaufe they were fo; even fuch as liv'd in Obedience to the Laws of the feveral Countries, where they refided, but in Point of Confcience, and for the Salvation of their Souls, neither cou'd, nor wou'd fubmit to *Popery*, *Tyranny*, *Idolatry*, and *Superftition*, Companions always infeparable; witnefs the bloody, barbarous and moft flagitious Maffacres of *Ireland*, *Paris*, the *Palatinate*, and the Hereditary Dominions of the Empire, with many others, not to mention the Bleffed Martyrs in the Reign of the *Popifh Queen Mary* here at Home; the Thoughts of which only, muft ever plunge the honeft well-meaning Subject into the deepeft Melancholy; and to find that there fhou'd be now amongft us bafe Men, en-

deavour-

deavouring to bring upon us the like
Woes, Cruelties, and Miseries, can't,
I hope, but fire you with the warmest
Resentments.

I must beg leave to observe to
you, that Rewards and Punishments
are the best and surest Support of
the Body Politick; and, as it has
been the fix'd Opinions of the greatest Divines and Statesmen; that Men
may be guilty of such Crimes in this
Life, as ought not to be forgiven
here; I must plainly tell you, that
all concern'd in the late Rebellion,
against the present Legislature, are
the highest Criminals of that kind;
the Forgiveness of Injuries, personal-
ly transacted between Man and Man,
is trivial, of a quite different and in-
ferior Nature, no ways relative to
the Case of these unnatural, rebelli-

ous Delinquents; nay, I will venture to affirm the Maxim is juftifiable, and good in many private Cafes, fuch as in *Sodomy*, or where a brutal Father fhall force, and enjoy the Body of his own natural Children, *&c.* in which, I think, no good Man, and Chriftian, can differ from me. And tho' thefe are hideous and fhocking Sins, but what are they, when you compare them to this Rebellion? Every Mufket was pointed at, and according to the known Tendency, and Conftruction of the Law, with an intent to murder the bleffed King, and glorious Family, and thereby deftroy the State. Can any atrocious *Papift*, or *Jacobite*, be fo corrupt, fo harden'd, carry fuch a brazen Front, as even to infinuate, that the leaft Tendernefs ought to be fhown the Criminals, I have fairly defcrib'd; when

fure

sure no Man, tho' never so Vitious,
dare openly, at least, assert, that the
minutest Indulgence shou'd be shown
to Delinquents, in the private Cases
abovemention'd.

I must also observe to you, That
the vulgar Notion of Mercy is false
and erroneous; it is in Compassion
to the Innocent, that Laws are made
to punish the Nocent; and it is the
highest Goodness and Mercy to the
upright, when the Almighty is pleas'd
so to destroy the Wicked, that no
more just Men may fall through the
Malice of their Hearts, and the Poi-
son of their Lips. King *James* the

Murderer, was pleas'd to make An-

"It ought; but shou'd he pardon him,
"and he repeat the Crime, it was his
"firm

" firm Opinion, that the Guilt then
" wou'd lie at his Door.". For a Man
to fay, that he is forry fuch *Traytors*
legally convicted are to die, is high-
ly Abfurd and Ridiculous ; he may,
with equal Folly, fay, that he is much
concern'd, that ever wholfome Laws
were enacted, than which, nothing
wou'd be more ftupid. This does
not debar every good Man from fhow-
ing a decent Contrition, that his Fel-
low-Creature. has merited the Penal-
ty of thofe necefary good Inftituti-
ons ; political Forgivenefs is in the
Soveraign. But then fuppofe after an
Amnefty, the prefent *Traytors* fhou'd
rebel again, at whofe Door muft the
Unhappinefs be ? Indeed, it's true,
that the Ignorant and Deluded can't
operate, when their Leaders and Se-
ducers are no more, than the Body
can act without the Head ; and for
my

my part, I have good Nature enough to Compound for that, and no lefs, were it in my Power. Thefe moft execrable Mifcreants, I hope, can't imagine in Reality, but fome reafona- ble Atonement fhou'd be made for Crimes of fo deep a Die; fome Satis- faction for the Blood of thofe gallant, brave Fellows, that at *Dunblain* and *Prefton*, fell in the glorious Caufe of God, their King, and Country, by the Hands of thefe *Rebels*; let them but confult the Widows and Father- lefs, the Mothers and Fathers having loft their Sons, that they barbaroufly have occafion'd; let them compofe their feveral *Juries*. Muft an in- jur'd Prince, and People, have no Redrefs for the vaft Sums expended, the Decay of Trade, and Confufion, for a while, it introduc'd? Can any Body fuppofe, that out of a Body of

about

about Twenty Thousand, such *Criminals*, a few *Calves-Heads*, to the *Northward*, and a brace of *Cods-Heads*, to the *Southward*, with the *Irish Head* upon *Temple-Bar*, of *Morrogan O Sullivan, alias* Captain *Silver*, are a sufficient Amends? Idle and preposterous! A Man may as rationally propose to satisfy the Nation's Debts, consisting of so many Millions Sterling, with a Bill of that Dog's, the *Pretender's*, endors'd by General *Mar*.

But before I leave you, pardon me, if I put you in Mind of an old *English* Proverb, *viz. When the* Fox *preaches, beware the* Goose. And I beg you to observe, how under the Pretence of Liberty and Property, as the *Papists* murder *Protestants* through religious Zeal, all the *Jacobites*, and disaffected *Desperado's* are railing, and

in-

inveighing against our Divine Legislature, upon the Introduction of a Bill, for a *pro tempore* Suspension of the *Triennial Act.* And take this as an unerring Standard with you, that whenever you find those *Traytors,* and their *Abettors,* convuls'd and dull, you have just Reason to be Gay and Chearful; and whenever they rejoyce, some Mischief is at Hand to all good Men.

The very Men I have been speaking of, even those, that, with all their Might, oppos'd this *Triennial Act,* when first brought into the House in the Reign of that Glorious Monarch King *William,* well knowing it wou'd effectually prevent the Return of King *James,* and *Popery, &c,* and *mutatis mutandis,* those same sort of *Gentry* oppose now, as strenuously the Suspen-

penfion of it, becaufe it will ftrengthen
our Alliances; our Confederates will
put an entire Confidence, and Truft
in us; our Trade will flourifh; all
Hopes of the *Pretender*, and his *Ad-
herents* will totally abate; the Minds
of the People be compos'd, and fet-
tl'd; the Gentlemen, and Commonal-
ty greatly eas'd from Expence, and
Hurry; much Confufion, and Tu-
mults obftructed, with many other
Advantages. But what may not a
People reafonably expect from fo Glorious a Monarch? So wife, and honeft a Miniftry? And from Two fuch
unparalell'd Houfes of Parliament?
I cou'd infinitely enlarge on this Occafion, and ftrictly keep within the
bounds of Truth, but having already
exceeded the ufual length of a Let-
ter, I can only affure you, that no
Man living, loves, and honours the
King,

King, the Church of *England*, as by Law eſtabliſh'd, and my Country, with more Zeal and Sincerity then,

Dear Countrymen,

Yours at all Commands,

E. L.

F I N I S.

King, the Church of England, as by Law establish'd, and my Country, with more Zeal and Sincerity than,

Yours at all Commands,

—————————————————

FINIS.